MW01297916

COACH 'EM UP

Going Beyond the "W" in Sports

JAY ZELLER

ISBN-10: 153099649X
ISBN-13: 978-1530996490

DEDICATION

To Rachelle for putting up with all the lonely nights in bed and being an ear when I needed to vent. You always supported my career and I always appreciated it even when I didn't say it. I couldn't have done any better in the wife and friend department. 143

To Jace, Emilee, and Kiley for being great kids. Everything I do is for your benefit. Keep doing great things in life. I can't wait to see what the future has in store for each of you. You guys are awesome!

To every assistant coach that has worked with me over the years. I appreciate you all more than you know. Thanks for dedicating so much time to our kids.

To all my former players for putting up with the craziness that I bring. You have impacted my career and my life more   than   you   will   ever   understand.   PFA!

CONTENTS

INTRODUCTION

During my final year as a coach I said, "I should write a book." I remember saying that over and over again to my friend and assistant coach, Jana Hammonds, that final year. I can't tell you how many times I've used that phrase during my coaching career. I think everyone has likely said those five words at some point in their career. I know I have worked with many coaches and teachers that have said that same phrase over the years. As educators and coaches, we often hear those words or have the idea to write a book when something very funny happens or, in many cases, when something negative happens that becomes the driving force behind the idea.

Most of the time those are empty conversation words. For me personally they were definitely said in conversation until recently. My drive to start writing was fed by anger and a negative experience. That was the fastest I have ever written ten pages. One day before I started back on the book I was reading over my words in order to get back in the flow. I realized that everything I had written was negative and pointless. Who was going to gain anything by reading those thoughts? I sure wasn't to gain anything. The thoughts on paper were not going to change the events of the past. Those thoughts certainly were not going to help anyone reading them, if anyone would even choose to read such garbage.

Ultimately, I found the positive in the time I had spent writing. You won't see any of those anger fed words in the pages to come. The medicine was in releasing the thoughts from my head and getting rid of them. I decided to move forward and write about some of the experiences during my career that can serve as tools to help other coaches. I trashed those first ten pages and started fresh.

My goal is to provide each of you with the strength to do the same as you move through your career. If you coach long enough you will have ups and you will have downs. Hold on tight to the highs and work diligently to get through the lows. Stay positive and have the mindset that nothing will ever be able to hold you down.

Here's to all of those times! I hope you find something valuable with the stories about my experiences and lessons learned that I chose to share with you from my coaching days.

#PFA

COACH 'EM UP

1
THE PATH TO COACHING

Sports have always been a major part of my life. As a kid, I tried football and basketball with little success at the team level. I could throw and kick a football very well but just couldn't get it done at game speed with huge guys chasing me. I could play horse with the best of them but that didn't seem to translate to the court. I was fairly successful early on in baseball. I could hit, catch and throw. I had two problems though. When I hit the ball, I couldn't seem to just drop the bat. I always threw it to the backstop, many times resulting in an out for throwing the bat. My other problem was as we grew older the ball started coming faster or it appeared to be coming directly at my head before it curved into the strike zone. Needless to say I stopped being productive at the plate. The one constant for me was soccer.

I first discovered my love of soccer as a kid playing in the Mesquite Soccer Association in Texas. Soccer was the one sport that just fit with my skill set. The more I played the more I excelled at the mental and physical part of the game. I played nearly from the time I could run until my family moved the summer before my eighth grade year. Unfortunately, the move to be closer to family meant being too far from a major city with a soccer league. Soccer would go away for the next six years.

Not one to quit, I used my soccer background to find a home on my high school football team. That's right. I was a kicker. I dabbled in other positions as needed but they weren't really my strength. High school football was my way of being involved and representing my school colors and town. I was a Brownsboro Bear and wore the Blue and Gold with great pride! What I didn't know at the time was that it would also provide me with my first look at coaching in a high school program. One could argue that the experience was my first coaching clinic. I was cataloging memories of coaches in the classrooms, at practices, in town, and of course on the game fields.

Changes were on the horizon. In February of my senior year, I entered the United States Air Force on the delayed enlistment program. I married my wife about two weeks after high school graduation and then went off to basic training in San Antonio, Texas in September of 1994. After basic training and Security Forces Technical School, I received orders to Barksdale Air Force Base in Bossier City, Louisiana. Why is this important? This was the real beginning of our family and my military enlistment but in keeping with the theme, this is where I found soccer again. Barksdale Air Force Base had intramural leagues for a variety of sports. Squadrons formed teams and registered to compete against other squadrons. I played soccer, flag football, and learned how to play volleyball from a great friend. I loved getting to compete in the various sports but for me this was an opportunity to continue my childhood passion. What began as a way to play soccer again led to a taste of coaching. There were no official coaches so several of us with a soccer background managed the team. For my wife this was the beginning of what would become her marriage to a coach.

Four years came and went. When my enlistment in the Air Force was complete, Rachelle and I moved back to East Texas with our six-month-old son. To support my family, I took a full time job as a private investigator instead of completing my college degree. It was about this time that I started working with a local soccer team that traveled about 40 miles to play in the Tyler Soccer Association's open league, a combination of club and recreational teams. After helping out with the team for a season I ended up taking on the task of coaching them for the next two years. I was young and inexperienced but I attended coaching clinics regularly through the state association to grow as quickly as possible. Looking back I can see how green I was but everyone has to start somewhere and who knows where I would be without this experience in my life.

After a couple of years of working and coaching, I decided that I wanted to finish my college degree and become a high school teacher and coach. I took nearly sixty hours at Louisiana Tech University while I was in the Air Force so I didn't have a lot left if I just put my mind to it. I worked part time and took a full load year round. I was attending every semester or mini session they offered. Once again life put me in the right place at the right time. My son was now five and playing on a soccer team with the son of our family friend. That friend just happened to be the head boys soccer coach in the town we were living in. My final semester of college was in the spring of 2003. My only class that semester was student teaching. I was able to get a student teaching position at Athens

High School and helped out with the boys soccer team. This was an invaluable experience for me. Coaching high school is much different than coaching a recreational or club team. There are so many other details off of the field that a coach handles, not to mention being able to balance the teaching assignment with the coaching assignment. I learned so much but the experience was priceless. I was doing everything a normal teacher and coach was doing except getting a paycheck.

I graduated in the spring of 2003 and sent my resume off to nearly every school in the state that had an open history and soccer position. Everything to that point in my life was about to pay off for me. I was offered and accepted the head boys soccer position at Lampasas High School. Now with three kids, Rachelle and I packed up and started our new life in Lampasas, Texas. It wasn't long before I found out just what *other assigned duties* meant! I was building a table in the garage one day during the summer before I began working and a strange truck pulled up in the driveway. I was introduced to the junior high athletic coordinator and learned that the junior high volleyball program was one coach short. Just like that, I became the seventh grade B team volleyball coach. I had a lot of fun learning with that group of young ladies that season and the experience would pay off before I was done coaching.

And so the coaching adventure began! I coached from 2003 to 2014 at four different high schools. The first half of my career was spent coaching boys, other than that first seventh grade volleyball season, but I finished up on the girls side of the house. I learned a lot during my tenure before deciding it was time to hang up my whistle for administration. Along the way I worked with a lot a great people and faced a number of challenges. Aligning myself with quality people, having a supportive family, and great friends made the challenges easier to conquer. I'm stronger because of the impact these people and challenges had on my life.

2
THE COACHING SPECTRUM

Honest Zeller time! There's nothing like starting with a bang and some honest evaluations of what a coach should be *and should not* be. For some, this will strike a nerve. Others will say AMEN brother! Regardless of which side you fall on, the point is to share the benefits of coaching to a level that exceeds those expectations we require of our players. The goal of this chapter is to provide an avenue of self-assessment and reflection for current and future coaches, head and assistants. The idea being to help coaches lead their programs and ultimately raise the standard simply by setting the tone with their own work ethic and actions.

I tend to place coaches somewhere on a spectrum between two vastly different categories describing high school coaches. I like to refer to these as the Program Coach and the Seasonal Coach. Admittedly, there's a wide gap in between the two and more often than not, coaches fall in the so-called gray area between them. If your job is to lead student athletes, the gray area isn't a bad place to be but it means there's room to grow personally and professionally. The goal is to identify, through honest self-evaluation and reflection, where you are on the spectrum. In doing so, you will also identify weaknesses, or areas that you can build on. Hopefully that process starts some internal reflection, which begins the movement toward the Program Coach.

So, what are these categories and how do I define them?

The Seasonal Coach

The Seasonal Coach is exactly what it sounds like. You've heard of seasonal employees during certain major shopping seasons. Businesses bring in part time help to assist in the additional workload during the busy season, like that of retail businesses around Christmas time. Most seasonal employees aren't invested in helping the company grow. They typically work fewer hours than their full time counterparts and their work ethic is not up to par due to knowing there's no future at the business. They are clock punchers just drawing a paycheck while it lasts.

A Seasonal Coach isn't much different. There are several reasons a coach would land on this end of the spectrum. Some have merit and those coaches will move up the spectrum quickly. Others need to find a different line of work or possibly just be an assistant coach under a strong leader until such time that they are ready to actually lead a program in a positive direction.

Coaches in this category are brand new to high school coaching. They often struggle with balancing the teaching and the coaching parts of their jobs. They may have coached outside of education and not be familiar with the school process. These coaches will likely struggle in the offseason time period as well as with some aspects of the job while they are in season. It is very important to provide brand new coaches with a solid mentor head coach that is willing to teach them the tricks of the trade. Athletic Coordinators and Athletic Directors should know who on their staff have the proven ability help mold and grow these coaches quickly. Mentoring is not a job for the negative veteran coach just because they've been doing it for so long. Find someone who is upbeat and has a real passion for what they do! A new coach should not be stagnant on the spectrum. They should be eager to learn and ultimately move quickly in the right direction.

Another example in this category is the coach who has been placed in that role as their second sport. This typically happens to assistant coaches and less to head coach positions. It does happen though, especially in smaller schools. An example might be one of the assistant football coaches being the head boys soccer coach. Often times in cases like this, the coach doesn't have a solid background in the second sport, soccer in this example. This is a tough position for that coach to be in. There's been no long-term investment in this sport. Many times they try and do the best they can in season but then it's back to their main sport when the season is over. Hopefully they fall in the Program Coach category for their first sport and just don't understand how to be an effective second sport coach. This is not an excuse though. The student athletes in the second sport deserve the opportunity to grow and build the program. They will need a head coach that is committed to the growth of the individual players as well as the entire program.

The most worrisome example in this category is the clock punching coach. These coaches typically aren't organized in any area of the job and have a poor work ethic. They are rarely prepared for practice or do the same practice over and over with little to no thought about the big picture. Their paperwork is incomplete or well behind schedule. They are still trying to fill holes in their schedule right before their season starts because they didn't plan ahead or work the phones/emails of fellow coaches to find games. Many times this results in several open dates for their players because it's too late to find games. These coaches are non existent in the offseason and don't participate in professional development to improve. They do just enough to get by during their season, if that even. Many Seasonal Coaches only attend sub varsity games if they play right before their varsity game. There is very little interaction with the sub varsity group. The list could go on and on. In my humble opinion, this coach should not be leading a program. Maybe, with some guidance and direction from a great head coach, they would do better as an assistant coach until they show major signs of improvement.

Ultimately, if you fall into this category, or you are in the grey area close to it, just take some time to evaluate yourself. You might be a rookie head coach and just need time to learn everything required of you. That's okay as long as you are working on your growth in that position while developing your players. Identify coaches at your school who are doing it right and take the time to visit with them and soak it all in. That doesn't mean that everything they do in their program will work in yours. Listen and learn. You may end up modifying things they do well so they work for your program. Also, create a network of coaches in your sport. Coaches by nature enjoy coaching. That includes players and fellow coaches. I learned a lot from visiting with coaches that were opponents and also when I was scouting. I watched the coaches a lot during games I was scouting. The main focus is developing yourself so you can be the very best for your players. If you do a good job of that then you will in turn be doing right by your players. They will gain from your growth because you will be more prepared and knowledgeable.

The Program Coach

The Program Coach is quite the opposite of the Seasonal Coach. This coach is not perfect and will always have room to grow but they are committed to their own growth and the growth of their players and program. This coach likely started off in the gray area closer to the Seasonal Coach because of their inexperience with the duties of a head coach position in a high school.

Unlike the seasonal employee just punching a clock, this type of employee quickly rises through the ranks and becomes well respected by their colleagues. The great aspect of the seasonal employee example is that a seasonal employee, with great work ethic and desire, can outshine their counterparts and earn a full time position. For high school coaches this example may mean opportunities to advance to larger programs, gaining the respect of the coaching community, or simply building a well respected program. The most satisfying benefit is doing right by your players and building a program.

So, what does it take to be a Program Coach? For starters, I should clarify that this isn't an all or nothing category. Some of the examples aren't possible for a variety of reasons when it comes to coaching high school sports. For the most part though if you're doing it right and putting forth great effort then you are doing what's best for your athletes and building a strong program. In the end, that's what it's all about.

Knowledge is power! Having a solid background is very important to being an effective head coach but it doesn't stop there. You should be seeking professional development opportunities every chance you get. There are several reasons this is important and these will be discussed in greater detail later in this book.

A coach on this end of the spectrum is well organized. Whether it's for practices, games, or the administrative part of the job, this coach has a plan with a goal in mind.

Practices must be planned! That means they are thoughtful and engage athletes in a variety of activities that most likely flow with the theme for the session or day. A well-balanced practice builds on the prior drill to continue through to the team goal. Basically, start small, or with the individual player, and continue to build the session all the way to the team level. Great coaches understand how to keep players active in the practice. There is less standing around waiting on their turn in the activity. There are many ways to accomplish this. An example could be creating several small groups to have every player active. If space or supervision are concerns then create several groups and rotate them through down time activities so those not involved in the desired drill are still working. An example of that might be having a one minute, fast paced, drill with two competing groups involved while one *resting* team performs core strengthening exercises while they are off. Rotate each group so they are active for two minutes and *resting* for one minute. Many times coaches perform drills like this and the group that's off is just standing around talking. Get the most out of players and build a sense of teamwork by having everyone working at the same time and taking water breaks together. Team breaks also allow coaches that are working alone to transition between drills while the players are getting water instead of having them stand around waiting for you.

Organized coaches have done their homework prior to games. Know your team! Who are your starters and how do you manage playing time? I can't stress enough the importance of planning for everything when it comes to game management. I kept several small dry-erase boards in my office that I always sat and talked through game management with my assistant coaches or even worked through it by myself. This is a great way to think through your starting lineup and how to manage the players on the bench. You never know what's going to happen in a game and being ready with substitutes in mind for each position or player is crucial.

Another piece of game organization is knowing your opponent. Take the time to scout as often as possible or trade game video within your coaching network. Scouting requires extra time and often means spending another night away from home or taking a personal day at work. This is one of the commitment pieces that will keep many coaches on the Seasonal Coach end of the spectrum. It's taxing for sure but the time commitment is all part of being the leader of a program. Side note, this is another reason to build a network. Many coaches will not give game video of their coaching friends away, even if they really need to trade. Build your network and be good to it! Late in the season it becomes harder and harder to scout games for most sports because the majority of sports have small staffs. Coaches are more willing to trade game video to help their team out late in district competition and in the playoffs. This is tough without a network.

The Program Coach also takes care of all administrative tasks in a timely manner. These tasks include completing bus requests for all away games, managing the program inventory and budget, creating a competitive schedule that challenges the program, as well as other details. You must be able to meet deadlines to ensure you are prepared for everything. The last thing you need on your way out to practice is for your Athletic Coordinator to say you missed something and they need it immediately. This will create undo stress and your players see the chaos it creates. Take care of business!

Start building a competitive schedule early. I always started building my schedule as soon as my season was over, and in some cases before it ended. It seems crazy to end in April and immediately start finding games for the following January but you get the games you want when you start early. My schedule for the following school year was always done before leaving for summer break. Mismanaging your schedule will leave holes on game nights or means you are forced to fill a date with a team that is well below your talent level.

This takes away from the growth of your players and is a direct reflection of your lack of preparation. If you are a first year head coach, or have just taken a new job, make sure you know the area before creating your schedule. Don't assume that because a school is in the same classification that you should be scheduling them for scrimmages or non-district games. I made this mistake once and learned quickly to rely on information from my network about teams I wasn't sure about before scheduling them. In my case, my team was far superior than the team we were scrimmaging and as a result neither team benefitted from the scrimmage.

The Program Coach knows how to manage the offseason. Each high school sport is a little different. It depends on when your sport begins and ends. Have a plan for the time your program isn't in season. For me this was August through Thanksgiving break and from April through the end of the school year. My first offseason, August through November, was very different than the months after my season was over. The focus at the beginning of school was to get to know what I had and what we needed as a program. That meant observing the freshman players and new transfers. It also meant gauging the returners, mentally and physically. I always liked to hit the ground running, unless it was my first year at the school. After the first year there's no need for a get to know each other day. Players knew the expectations for day one of school and we got after it. I believe that it sends a message that I'm excited about getting the season started and that we are going to work to accomplish our goals.

The first offseason, I referred to it as our preseason, was about getting on track mentally and physically. We were less focused with our team play early on as we were with everyone committing to working hard for themselves and each other. We began our mindset in the fall. If you're in season and just starting to discuss and work on mentality it's too late. At that point, you're likely discussing it because there's an issue. Don't wait for your game day to drill mental focus, teamwork, and competitiveness!

Build from there based on your observations and discussions with your assistant coaches. What does the team need to get to the next level? Don't get caught up in the theory that just because you are returning most of your varsity players that all will be well. Teams change from year to year in high school. The talent will likely be the same or better but they could be in a completely different spot mentally from when you last worked with them in May or June. I learned to appreciate and fear large senior classes. You just never know what senior year is going to do to them. The majority are not impacted. They are great leaders and are focused on doing what is necessary for a great final season. Some come back with what many call senioritis. Senioritis is a killer!

I say all of that just to prove that a year in and year out routine is not best. Be observant to what your program needs. The offseason routine you've had for the last few years may be the complete opposite of what your group actually needs to be successful.

My actual offseason, the one in April and May, was a mixture of what I believed the returning group for the next year needed and a little fun. I was very demanding and had high expectations for my players in season, well all year but in season was when it all came to a point. I felt like the players needed me to take a step back just a bit after the season. I learned over the years that them seeing me smile, as they would say, and have fun was very impactful and ultimately paid dividends down the road. We still worked hard on the areas that I thought the returning group needed to focus on for the following season but I built in fun days. These were also the times where I listened to them a little more. I would be more willing to alter plans if I felt like they needed it. Know your leaders and listen to them. They will bring the mood of the group to you. Evaluate the information and make wise decisions. For me, a fun competition day in May instead of going to the weight room was great for morale. I'm not saying that should happen every day but be willing to change your plans. I promise it will pay off more than that weight workout or drill day will!

One of the most important aspects of leading a program is making sure your focus is on the whole program. Many coaches get caught up in the varsity mentality during the season, and sometimes year round. Program Coaches are there for their sub varsity teams. This can't always happen but when one of your sub varsity teams is playing or practicing and the varsity is not, the head coach should be there. You should be there for many reasons, most importantly because this is your future and they deserve your attention. This is a great time to relax, observe, and teach the younger players. You get to coach, both your sub varsity players and assistant coaches, in a setting that doesn't have the same level of stress as the varsity competitions. Balance high expectations with their need to see that you care about their growth. Many sub varsity players are nervous around the head coach. Take these opportunities to be the calming force for them.

* * *

Take the time to figure out where you are on the spectrum. You owe it yourself to honestly evaluate where you are. More importantly, you owe it to your players and your program as a whole, including future players, to do so. It's okay to be in the gray area or even close to the Seasonal Coach end. The key is make sure you're always growing and working on moving closer and closer to the Program Coach side of the spectrum. In education, we use the phrase be a lifelong learner. That goes for coaching as well. Never settle for what you already know. Keeping building on that knowledge! Doing so will no doubt make you a better leader for your program and campus.

3
THE COACHING DYNAMICS

Each coaching position has a specific role in a program. In order for the program to be successful each coach has to understand his or her role and work so the system as a whole functions together. As I reflect back on each of these roles in a program I am able to see the successes and the failures. I am able to see why some things worked and others didn't. I see when the roles worked together seamlessly and the effect it had on the program and visa versa. Don't allow your situation to dictate your opportunity. Take control of your situation and work diligently with the team, coaches and players, so that the program functions as a unit.

Role of the Head Coach

As a head coach you are the captain of your ship. It is your job to navigate the program through the calm waters as well as the rough waters. The position calls for a person with great vision and patience. It takes a person with the ability to build others. The wrong captain will lead the program into the eye of the storm.

Naturally, head coaches tend to think about themselves and their players. You must be intentional about taking care of your assistant coaches. Keeping them happy and healthy is important, not only for them but for the program and campus.

Head coaches play a major role in the growth of their assistant coaches, or they should. Don't wait until the end of the school year, when you're completing evaluation paperwork, to discuss areas of improvement or ways to gain more knowledge. That is a clear sign of a head coach being too close to the Seasonal Coach side of the spectrum. Work with them throughout the year. Take them under your wing. It doesn't need to be official, with documentation of areas to improve. Taking the time to talk, and teach, will go a long way in the staff relationship but also in the total growth of the assistant coach and program. Remember, your assistant coaches are teaching the future of your program. Don't forget to coach them up as well!

It is the job of the head coach to lay the foundation for the assistant coaches. It doesn't matter if your program is his or her first or second sport, your job is provide them with opportunities to grow. To do that, you have to have a vision. You must have a vision for yourself, a vision for your assistant coaches, and a vision for your program. Without the complete vision you will be walking as individuals down a dark path. There may be light in places along the way but ultimately you are walking slowly, feeling your way through the darkness, down much of the path. Use every light switch available to you to illuminate the path.

Over the years I have developed a pretty good sense of what an assistant coach needs. Regardless of their coaching background or experience in that particular sport, an assistant coach needs guidance. They need a direction. An assistant coach needs the vision. That vision, and the vision for the entire program, must come from the head coach. Not only should they develop a vision but also the head coach must *share the vision.* A vision not communicated to the program is just an individual's dream. I don't know about you but I have never seen a vision for a program fulfilled overnight, much less while coaches or players were fast asleep. The fulfillment of a vision, a programs success, all of that can only be accomplished if everyone in the program has a clear understanding of the vision and of their role within the vision. When all of those moving parts come together and the work is put in day in and day out, practice after practice, then and only then will the opportunity to be successful present itself. Maybe you caught that. The *opportunity* to be successful will present itself.

There are no guarantees in life. Whether it's an individual or team, it may take a handful of opportunities before you find success. The vision is the key. Keep after it. Reflect on the missed opportunity and go back to work so the program is ready when the next opportunity presents itself.

Like others, the stories that I share here come from my experiences and from watching and learning from my network. I can honestly say that along the way I have provided a vision for many of my assistant coaches. A few of them have become head coaches. I love getting to be a small part of their journey. Having said that, I am haunted by the couple of assistant coaches that I didn't share the vision with.

Remember, we don't always get the assistant coach that we want or need for our program. It is our job, our duty as head coaches to prepare them. Get them ready as quickly as possible to coach in a sport they may not be familiar with. Coach 'em up as we say. I knew this my entire career but I was selfish. I didn't complain to administration that I didn't have what I needed. Instead I put the blinders on for how they could help me and I just did it myself. That mindset was wrong on so many levels. First, my job was to mentor the assistant coach. I needed to take him or her under my wing and prepare them as if they were beginning a career in that sport. I should have paved a clear path for how they would develop in year one, year two, and so on. I should have shared the vision and allowed him or her to become an important part of the program. Second, I failed the team I was leading at the time. As coaches, we are to teach beyond the game. We should be teaching life lessons. Kids are very observant. They see the relationship between the coaching staff and easily determine whether or not it's a healthy one. Finally, my mindset about the situation wasn't healthy for me. I placed far too much pressure and stress on myself. You see the burden of the head coach is to create the blueprint for the program, not to set every stone on the path. A programs path should be a partnership between the coaching staff, the players, and yes, even the parents.

Be the mentor for the first year coach right out of college. Be the mentor for the assistant coach coming to you from another sport. Also, be the mentor for the veteran assistant coach in your sport. As a head coach in a high school program you will no doubt be charged with mentoring and leading assistant coaches from a variety of backgrounds.

I suggest that you meet with each coach as soon as possible after they are hired, or if you are coming into a new school, to evaluate what lies ahead of you. You will need to know what their history in your sport is so you know how to mentor them. You need to know if they are new to education or a veteran educator. You are tasked with coaching them up in your sport so they are ready to assist the program. You are also tasked with making sure they understand how to manage their two jobs, athletics and academics. Provide them the opportunities for professional development in your sport. Tell them about the various associations for coaches and how to become a member and attend their conferences. Scratch that. Don't just tell them about the opportunities; invite them to come with you.

Another very important piece to the growth of an assistant coach is allowing them to coach. I struggled with this a couple of times in my career. I understand the mindset of I have to coach both teams because my assistant doesn't know what he or she is doing. I've been there folks. While that may be true during the early phases of the partnership, it shouldn't be the case for long if the head coach will take the time to model and coach 'em up. Work with the assistant coach. Have them mirror you. It's important for an assistant coach to see what you do and hear what you say. That will help create a common message in the program when you are able to turn them loose. Talk to them before and after a practice so they know the plan and then are a part of the reflection. Your assistant coaches will grow faster, regardless of their background, if you are supporting that growth. Begin to switch roles so you are now mirroring them. Maybe that starts with a certain segment of the practice but in time builds to an entire practice.

I believe it is very important to have a practice plan for all coaches at all levels. I know many head coaches are able to create a mental practice plan and it works very well for them. I am of the opinion that you just never know what is going to happen in a session that distracts you or causes you to lose focus. This is even more important for an assistant coach. My practice plans included not only what I was doing throughout the practice but also when I was doing them. In most cases, I also took the time to script groups and teams for a practice. This will save time during your practice. Model that for your assistant coaches. A practice totally planned and scripted is most efficient.

There are years when you have a staff that is knowledgeable and experienced. I've known some head coaches to shy away from this type of staff because it intimidates them. They would rather have the inexperienced coach and complain about not having someone to coach because it's comfortable to them. The inexperienced coach likely won't challenge any decisions or strategies. This is simply the wrong attitude on so many levels. This mentality is that of a seasonal coach who is only in it for himself or herself. They are looking for an easy reward instead of working hard throughout the process.

If you're fortunate enough to have an assistant coach that is knowledgeable in your sport use them. Allow them to coach. Allow them to be a part of the discussions about the direction of the team. There is no need in carrying the burden of the process on your shoulders. When you work together with your assistant coaches and you allow them the flexibility to provide input and plan the whole program will benefit. Ideas that you once had can be discussed and built upon so they become even better or they were great ideas that have now been validated by someone else with the knowledge to provide valuable information. A staff that works together will reap the rewards of the teamwork and thought that goes into the process.

Even better than the relationship among the staff is what the body language of the staff is modeling for the team. We often forget that we expect the players to be a team and work well together but sometimes we don't lead the way. I promise you your athletes know whether or not your coaching staff gets along or not. Even if you don't show it in public they can sense it. They see the relationship and how much rope the head coach allows the assistant coach. They see the head coach making all of the decisions or they see the head coach walking over to the assistant to discuss strategy. That makes a huge difference.

That staff relationship also shows the players the level of respect the head coach has for the assistant. The players are far more likely to follow an assistant coach that they know the head coach believes in rather than one that the head coach shuns. Imagine what would happen if you were not able to attend a practice or a game for some reason and the players didn't have confidence in the assistant. That practice or game would not be good and it would not be because you weren't there. It would be because of the image and mindset that you created in all of the sessions and days leading up to that event. Prepare your team to be successful. Prepare your coaches to be successful.

Role of the Assistant Coach

The unsung hero! Assistant coaches are often times overworked and under appreciated. They are the easiest people to forget about in a program. As an assistant coach, whether you are acknowledged or overlooked, your job is to keep grinding. Keep grinding for yourself. Keep grinding for the athletes. Keep grinding for the program. And yes, keep grinding for the head coach. You do it because it is the job. It's what a coach does. Coaches put theirs heads down and go to work. The more you grind the more your efforts will be noticed and appreciated.

Assistant coaches are not exempt from the coaching spectrum. They should be evaluating where they fall on the spectrum and constantly working to build on their own future. They have a huge responsibility to themselves and the program they are assigned to. Your task is to work hard day in and day out to move through the gray area. As you grow and get better, each day you move closer and closer to the Program Coach side of the spectrum. That growth will provide opportunities for you to advance your career and one day become a head coach, an athletic coordinator, or even an administrator. The sky's the limit but it's up to you and nobody else to get yourself there.

Plugging in high school coaches to open positions is often very interesting and controversial. Many schools require assistant coaches, and sometimes head coaches, to coach two different sports. Naturally, this means that one program is getting a knowledgeable assistant coach while the second sport, in many cases, is receiving a coach with little to no knowledge on the sport. This can work out if the two sharing head coaches work together to find the right person for the job, then cooperate with each other during the year, and of course if the assistant coach makes every effort to support and grow in each position.

Each coaching position has an important role in the success of the program. It does not matter whether you are the head coach or the assistant coach; you have a crucial place in the program. It does not matter if that assignment is your field of expertise or not, you have a crucial place in the program. Coaches, players, parents, and your administrators are depending on you to take full advantage of the opportunity to model successful behaviors.

Unfortunately, I can speak from experience as it relates to the working relationship between head coaches and assistant coaches. I have been the head coach who had the attitude of defeat because I was *stuck* with someone who knew nothing about my sport. I have also been the assistant coach in my second sport that worked hard but *felt* unappreciated and undervalued. Ultimately, this feeling impacted my effectiveness as a coach. In each case, my attitude inhibited my opportunity to grow personally and to help others grow.

As a head coach I have been on both sides of ensuring the growth of assistant coaches. I spent all but one year of my coaching career as a head coach in my sport. Every year I had a second, and once even a third coaching assignment. That meant I was an assistant coach in someone else's program. This provided me with the valuable understanding of what it's like to be an assistant coach. It also showed me firsthand what I did and did not want to be as a head coach.

First and foremost, the role of an assistant coach is to work hard. Work hard for the program. Work hard for the athletes in the program. Work hard for the coaching staff. Work hard for yourself. You see no matter how knowledgeable you are in a particular sport hard work will overcome anything. Hard work will lead to faster growth. Hard work will mask some of the unknown. We've all heard the phrase fake it till you make it. Fake it every day until you make it. That means coming in early and studying the practice plan or asking questions of the other coaches on staff. Go over that drill one more time so you have it down when the athletes are performing.

Be a sponge. Whether you are required to or not, go to the other practices of that particular sport when you get the opportunity. Listen to the coaches to pick up on a common language. Watch the drills and see how the coaches interact and position themselves. Read their body language. Be attentive during games. Watch the movement of players. Watch the coach and listen to the coaching adjustments. Doing this will increase your understanding and knowledge. You will learn your role and that of the each player on the field or on the court.

Offer your help during camps. This is important but especially if this is your second sport. Many coaches work their second sport and then return to their first sport mindset. Unintentionally, they quickly forget or lose the gains made and end up coming back the next season having to start all over. Working, or even being present at camps will help regain the information and prepare you for the upcoming season. It also puts you in front of the athletes and future athletes that you will be coaching. They will see you more and more as a coach of that sport instead of a *helper*.

Ask questions! Only you know what you don't know. Ask. The head coach, and other staff members for that matter, doesn't always know what you don't understand or need help with. If you see or hear something that doesn't make any sense you need to care enough about the program and your own growth to find the answer. I promise you a head coach will appreciate the inquiry. It shows that you are invested in his or her sport and want to be there. Ask for opportunities to go to clinics or conferences. Ask about attending the team camps in the summer.

The main take away from the roles of assistant coaches is to constantly grow. Growing each day will benefit you, it will benefit the program, and ultimately each athlete in the program will benefit.

They may not benefit from your sport knowledge but your work ethic and desire to grow will be noticeable and something to model for their growth in life after athletics.

4
COACHING THE COACH

Professional development. Two words that often kill the moods of educators, teachers and coaches alike, who are not in the right frame of mind. Admittedly, I was at the front of that line for far too long. It wasn't until I changed my mindset and focused on my own personal growth that I found value in spending the time to grow in professional development versus wasting the time going to professional development. Put another way, the old me was obligated to go because my employer made me. Whether that was the week of in-service before the first week of school, district convocation, or other professional development sessions needed, I was going because I *had to*. That negative mindset led to years of minimal personal and professional growth because I didn't take advantage of the opportunities that were staring me directly in the face. The opportunistic person seizes those chances to learn and enters the learning with a positive mindset because they *want to* grow. They are eager to build upon themselves in order to better guide those they come in contact with daily. Powerful! Opportunity versus obligation. Want to versus have to. If nothing else comes from this, my sincere hope is that you don't waste another second in the obligation phase of life. Opportunity is so sweet!

I allowed many opportunities to pass me by but thankfully I came in contact with the right people. Oddly enough this group of people were the very ones I had spent years avoiding at all cost. Administrators! I ran away from them mentally, and maybe even physically at times, because I wasn't ready for what they had to offer me. I saw them as an opponent instead of a coach, or mentor. They were there for me, and others, but I didn't allow them in.

I have a strong group of administrators at Mansfield High School, in Texas, to thank for my growth as an educator, a coach, and as a person. They were all unique individuals and each brought a little something different to the table. Each one of them had something, a lot of things actually, that I needed. The greatest thing that ever happened to me was actually one of my worst days. Finally an honest person and a strong leader came along and punched me in the gut. That became the sweetest beating of my life, figuratively speaking of course. I'll never forget that spring day in 2011. Here's what I left that meeting with. Keep in mind these are not the words said specifically, they were much more graceful and sincere, but this is my interpretation of how that conversation went:

You are not living up to your potential. You are not only failing yourself but you are failing the kids and our campus.

As I walked down the hall after leaving the office I was repeating that message over and over in my head. I returned to my classroom and sat down at my desk. My head is spinning at this point. I have always cared about my work and the way I do things. I paid attention to detail and completed tasks. I was someone you could always count on to help others and was definitely respectful. I did all of those things well but I neglected to honestly reflect on my work and therefore wasn't able to see that I wasn't growing. I was doing just enough to comfortably get by day to day. As I sat there and truly reflected on the way I approached my job up to this point, I realized that I was losing the battle, not because I didn't have the tools necessary but because I had been unwilling to use them. I have always been a competitor and always will be. For me, this was exactly what I needed to get me out of my comfort zone. This was the wake up call that I could be better personally and professionally.

I went to work! I don't mean that in the sense of my actual employment. I still did that; I just did it better and with more purpose. No, I mean I went to work on me! I'll never forget that afternoon, nor should I. I became more intentional about everything. I sought out advice on my classroom lessons from other teachers, I was eager to have conversations with teachers around me instead of being the loner down the hall, and most importantly, I got serious about growth. I started talking to my administration about opportunities. Remember, not long ago I was avoiding them like the plague. Now I wanted to see them and pick their brains.

Later that fall I did the unthinkable, for the old me anyway. I started planning and researching how I could go back to school for my Masters in Educational Administration. Going back to school could have been a financial setback for my family. I just had one problem with that excuse. I was a Veteran and a Texas resident. All this time I had the Hazelwood Act in my back pocket. The Hazelwood Act provides one hundred and fifty college hours, tuition free, to Texas Veterans. I knew all about this opportunity but I was comfortable in who I was back then. Not anymore! The old me would have said you don't have time to take that on. You have a family, you teach, and you are a head soccer coach and assistant volleyball coach at a 6A high school. When are you going to do this? I laugh at the old me now. I completed all of the paperwork and applied at Lamar University. I started the Master's program almost one year to the day after my principal had the meeting with me. I was more driven to succeed than I had ever been before. I started the program in April of 2012 and completed it in September of 2013. By the time I graduated in December I had not only completed all of the coursework for graduation but I had also completed all of the certification classes required and the Principal's Exam for the State of Texas.

It is very tough to admit failure, especially when you put it in black and white for all to see. That story of personal failure is a valuable tool for me. That day still burns strong in my heart and mind. It keeps me from getting comfortable again. My hope in sharing one of my personal failures here is that it will resonate with those of you that need a similar gut punch. You see the greatest part of this story is that it's no longer a failure story. That day I was offered an opportunity and I took hold of it and haven't let go to this day. I've learned that that is the difference between winners and losers. Winners are willing to work! Winners are willing to test their comfort zone! Winners don't turn back when faced with adversity! Don't miss this one. This is important for all of you leaders out there. Winners don't demand excellence of others while taking easy street. No, winners are leading the pack. Setting the bar of excellence for others to grab on to!

Professional development. Back to those two words. You see, before that gut punch that changed my approach, I attended lots of professional development sessions for my education career and many more for my coaching career. I approached each type differently. Yes, in many ways, I was in fact the stereotypical coach.

I mentioned earlier that professional development was an obligation for me. I went and sat through them. I wasn't drawing plays or playing tic-tac-toe with a fellow coach but I wasn't engaged. When I look back at how I approached coaching clinics and conferences, I don't think I was much better. Honestly, I was there because I chose to be there but was I there mentally, or physically. I can remember thinking or commenting to friends that this session isn't good at all. Or, this clinic was a waste of time. I thought I was locked in as a coach but even that part of me wasn't taking full advantage of the opportunities in front me. I tell you those things to stress to you the importance of getting yourself ready for opportunity to knock. Get your mind in the right place today. Seek opportunities to grow personally and professionally. Wake up in the morning ready to be different each day and allow yourself to grow. When you do those things, when your open your mind to new possibilities, then you will be show up engaged and on fire to learn.

Where do I go? What do I do when I get there? Coaches have many ways of obtaining professional development. The key is going to a variety of them in order to expose yourself to different types of messages. Your growth opportunity might be talking the coach in the adjacent office about his or her program. Don't restrict yourself to spending time only with those that coach the same sport as you. You are closing the door to opportunity if you do.

Building a Network

Possibly the most important form of professional development is building a network of fellow coaches. I can't tell you how many friends I made through the years just going to clinics or getting to know other coaches on my campus or in the district my program was in. Those connections were crucial to my growth. I spent hours speaking with coaches in one of our offices, on the phone, texting, or emailing back and forth to discuss situations that one of us was having. It doesn't matter whether you are the one giving the information or if you are receiving the information. The power is in the conversation. Both parties are processing and discussing a situation and because of the dialog, both are growing.

This wasn't an easy thing for me to do. By nature, I am very shy. I don't initiate conversation very often, especially if I'm in an unfamiliar setting. So going to a coaching clinic with hundreds, if not thousands, of new faces is awkward for me. Looking back, I see the amount of missed opportunities in all of the clinics and conferences I attended. Instead of stepping outside my comfort zone to make it a point to meet new people, I stayed in my shell and was just there. I was present but not fully present. I was taking advantage of an opportunity to grow but I wasn't taking full advantage of the opportunity. I was cheating myself and, quite possibly, others just like me. What if I had made that bold move and introduced myself to a fellow coach, seemingly also there alone? What if we formed a new friendship and what was once one person at a clinic nervous to open up became two, formerly nervous, people with newfound confidence. There is no doubt that there is power in fellowship and of course power in numbers. Two quickly becomes four. Four becomes five or six. And so on, and so on until one day you show up to clinics across the state, or even nation, and immediately have a community of people comfortable in there position there and eager to grow.

Early in my coaching career I had a small handful of coaches that I spoke to on a semi regular basis. If you're like me the only way to evolve and begin to grow your network is to be intentional about conversation at games and attend clinics of like-minded people.

What do you mean, be intentional about conversation at games? Some of you are thinking that by greeting an opposing coach with a wave or a handshake that you're doing that. You are cheating yourself and you are cheating that coach. All coaches should have a mental schedule in their head for their pregame routine, if not written or typed.

Most arrive at the game site a few minutes earlier than the start of the warm up. My suggestion is to add at least ten minutes to that schedule. Arrive early and allow your players to tend to their needs. During that time go introduce yourself and force a conversation. Very few people will walk away from you after the handshake if there's a conversation. If you don't know what to talk about just start small. The easiest is always asking them how things are going or talking about what might be big news in your specific sport for the area. Congratulate them on a big win. Do whatever it takes to strike up the conversation. Having said that, I urge you not to begin with something negative. The point in this is to build yourself and others. Don't waste this time complaining about parents or officials. Really get to know them and their program. By doing this every year, depending on the sport of course, you're going to gain anywhere from ten to thirty plus contacts. Some of those contacts will turn into friendships.

The beauty of this model of building a network is those new friends have a different network. The two networks merge and instantly grow in size at clinics or conferences. You will no doubt run into many of those new contacts when you attend clinics. They will likely be talking to another friend. Walk up and greet your friend and then introduce yourself to your newest contact. Bam! Your network is growing simply because you made time for conversation before a game. From there it just snowballs.

I have a great example of the power of extending your network. I finished my coaching career in the Dallas/Fort Worth area. That was my main network. The group I saw and spoke to most often. The rest of the state was my extended network that I either spoke to at conferences, the state tournament, or via text or email. I was at clinic in San Antonio one year, probably two years before getting out of coaching. When I arrived and entered the clinic I was greeted by a friend of mine from the DFW area. He was standing with a coach from the Houston area that he had become good friends with. I had never met him but knew of him. We began talking and as you know by now, each of our networks grew by one. How's that special? A few years after I met the coach I was an assistant principal at high school in the DFW area and we had an opening for a head soccer coach. Being a former soccer coach, I was heavily involved in the candidate reviews and interview process. Remember the network! This coach emailed me directly with an interest in the position. What's different about that than another candidate emailing? That connection several years early put a face and personal connection to a piece of paper. That network and the manner in which the network grew had an impact on where that piece of paper landed. Grow your network!

The job scenario is just one benefit of the network. Build your network for a variety of reasons. There's real power in building relationships!

Take Full Advantage of Learning Opportunities

Sports are always evolving. We attend professional develop to stay current in our chosen sport and to grow within our profession. Clinics and conferences provide multiple opportunities to learn. These opportunities present themselves in the form of lectures, field/court sessions, books, and of course the network. Don't limit yourself to just one or two of those opportunities. Experiencing them all will put you in the right frame of mind to take full advantage of every opportunity that comes your way.

Depending on the type of clinic you're attending, you may have a choice between several different sessions during each segment or there's just one session. If you have the choice of several, pick the one the best suites the needs of you and/or your program. Many of the clinics I attended offered two sessions per hour. I wanted to get the most out of the clinic so I used my network. One of the first things I did at a clinic was dive into the network. From there we developed a plan to attend different sessions so we covered them all. We were using our network to take full advantage of our learning opportunity. The real beauty of this method was teaching each other the lessons learned in each session. How much better can it get? The sharing of that new information then prompted a dialog about how it could be applied to our programs. Growth was happening!

I think in high school sports we get stuck in a pattern of professional learning. Some of that is because of the schedules we must keep due to having a dual teaching and coaching assignment. Coaches typically attend their sport association's general clinic each year. I believe these clinics do a good job of mixing the information and presentations every year but generally speaking the format stays the same. Coaches also attend their sports state championship tournament. That's if they attend two functions each year. Some coaches, and the number is drastically less, attend three or more clinics each year.

My suggestion to you is to keep doing, or start doing, both the clinic and state tournament for your specific sport. Do those two but add another or even two more if feasible. In Texas, another option to add variety to your learning is attending the general state associations. There are two options. The Texas High School Coaches Association (THSCA) or the Texas Girls Coaches Association (TGCA). I'm guessing most if not all states have similar state associations. These will allow you to branch out and attend a sport session that you are not involved in.

Why waste my time attending a different sports session you say? Remember earlier I mentioned that part of your network could be sharing information with coaches down the hall. Those coaches are involved in sports other than yours. The value is not in the "X's and O's" so to speak. The value is learning how other coaches handle their program. How they manage their time and practice. How they manage their staff. Attend those other sessions with the mindset of grabbing a hold of concepts, not plays. Seeking wisdom, not strategy. Your goal is to learn and grow from others. Be open-minded. Take full advantage of every opportunity!

Another option for growth is to find great books that will have an impact on you personally and professionally. For most of my coaching career I only bought books that pertained to soccer development. For instance, books on technique or systems of play. That's great but I was limiting my potential by only working on my soccer mind. To reach my full potential I needed to hone my leadership skills. I needed to read about topics such as mindset, management, character development, and so on.

Time is valuable as a coach. You want to know that when you pick up a book there's value in it. How do you find great reads? You guessed it. Use your network. Establish an email chain to share great book titles or links to articles you've found. Use social media. Here's a good one for all of you forum coaches. Create a thread for growth opportunities in your forums. Share tidbits of why you liked the book or article to entice others. Use the resources that you use every day but use them for growth instead of just to chat or make jokes.

Keep chatting and making jokes with each other. That's very important for coaches to do after a stressful day. Just make an effort to branch out and really use those tools to grow.

Where else can you find growth opportunities? Many of you are going to take this as a joke. I understand that because I was there once too. Hear me out because there's value out there in what I'm suggesting. Remember; take full advantage of growth opportunities.

So what is it that's so crazy? Search your Regional Service Centers or the Internet for leadership type conferences. Search for conferences outside of sports conferences. The great part is that your principals will likely pay for these, assuming there's a cost, and provide your substitute. It's a different concept I know. It's foreign to the type of professional development coaches typically attend. What you have to keep in mind is that you do more than coach. You lead a group of student athletes but you also lead students in your classrooms. Not to mention the leadership and guidance you can bring back to share with your colleagues. When you branch out you grow more. Take the step outside of your comfort zone. Take full advantage of improving upon you.

Once you dive into this pool of growth there's no doubt that you are going to come across some that are more interesting, or valuable, than others. Whether you are attending clinics, conferences, or reading books you will always find some better than others. You may not always get information that you feel provides great value to you or your program. The important piece to these types of sessions becomes the internal dialog that goes on inside your head. You tend to think about why it wouldn't work or create a variation that would benefit your program. The benefit here is the critical thinking that is taking place. You will attend great professional development sessions, or clinics, through the years as well as some that are not so great. You are in control of the gains that you take away from them.

Your mindset is vitally important when attending any conference. We've all been to clinics or conferences that we didn't like. We've all attended sessions of clinics that we felt like were a waste of time. You need to be locked in whether it's good or bad. The person that sits for five minutes and then determines that something is worthless will miss something great. That's worth repeating. The person that sits for five minutes and then determines that something is worthless will miss something great. It's easy to drift off once your mind tells you this is meaningless. You get your phone out and start playing a game or using social media or even texting the coach across the room about how ridiculous this is. You're missing the mental dialog and critical thinking. Stay locked in. After all, you expect your players to be locked in at all times! A true leader is someone willing to go above and beyond his or her own expectations of others.

Again, like many other times, I say this because I have been there personally. Who knows what I have missed because I drifted away mentally when I felt like something didn't apply to me or wasn't any good. I may have come around years earlier had I been fully engaged.

Here's a story about a few words that helped reshape my life and my focus that I nearly missed because I was drifting in and out of a clinic. I was only half there mentally. Fortunately for me, the somewhat engaged half was listening just at the right time because I will never forget three words that I heard that day. You read that correctly. Three words! Those three words have had a great impact on my life and I believe many of the athletes who came through my programs lives as well.

You might be saying, "Three words changed your life? Man, you're living in a dream world if you think words control who you are." To that point I might agree with you to an extent. You see the words themselves don't change you. Your thought processes about the words change you. Your self-reflections about how you live up to the meaning of the words change you. Those things give the words their power. The power in the words comes from your mind and your heart.

The story. I was attending the Schellas Hyndman soccer clinic at SMU in the spring of 2008. I was excited about attending again. The previous year had been great. I'll be honest, for whatever reason this one didn't draw me in like before. I was present but not fully engaged. I was sitting through a session being presented by Bill Beswick, former sports psychologists for the English Nation team. I was in and out mentally, but mostly in during his session as I recall. I remember enjoying his accent and use of words. See how mentally focused I was. My attention was on the wrong things. Thankfully though, his accent kept my attention because if not for that I probably would not have heard these three words in his presentation to us. I don't remember the full context or anything other than these three words. He said, "Performance follows attitude." That triggered something and I remember writing that down on a pad of paper. "Performance follows attitude." I am so fortunate to have heard those words that day.

Stay locked in and take full advantage of every opportunity to grow! Don't miss your three words.

5
PERFORMANCE FOLLOWS ATTITUDE

I was coaching girls soccer when I first heard those powerful words from Bill Beswick. I don't know about your experience with coaching girls but I provided a lot of entertainment, and irritation, during those times. The girls would say that most of that entertainment was at my expense. I was crazy and they either got a good laugh out of it or had the here he goes again thoughts. The performance follows attitude concept was another of those opportunities for crazy Zell to emerge. I delivered that message over and over and over. I put it on shirts. I put it on newsletters. I put it in my email. I preached performance follows attitude. To a certain extent all coaches do, or should in one way or another.

A couple years later I had an opportunity and accepted the position of head girls soccer coach at Mansfield High School. You better believe I brought Bill's three words along with me. This was an interesting four years for me and the performance follows attitude mantra. It was here that those three words really came to life for me personally and professionally.

I came in and during that first year I realized that I might be at the right place at the right time. That's not to blow myself up as some coaching stud. I came into the best coaching position of my career but it was broken. I had players with near endless talent but the mindset, the attitude, was all wrong. That coaching clinic several years earlier and those three powerful words were about to not only impact me but an entire program. It was here that the brand became the vision. The brand was no longer a brand. It was no longer three words. The brand became a reality. You see I learned that I could put words on shirts, paper, and emails or preach them all I wanted but until we defined them and set a vision and applied them within our lives and our program, we would never achieve true success.

I was used to players with some talent but rich with heart, determination, and a commitment to each other. All of those qualities define a player who possesses the right attitude. The Lampasas and Kennedale boys teams often overachieved because the program meant something to them. We never made the playoffs and ended each year around .500, sometimes over and sometimes under. The beauty in their game was the constant desire to compete because they loved the game. Nobody was bigger than the team. My girls at Kennedale achieved great things because of their drive and family mentality. They competed in a larger classification and had never been to the playoffs in program history. Before I left for the Mansfield job, that Kennedale team hit the map and went to the playoffs two times and won their first playoff game in a season where their commitment to do something special ended in a 19-4-4 season. Those teams had something greater than talent could ever bring. Their determination was greater than their talent. Their heart conquered their mind when it said they couldn't win. They had the attitude of champions.

That first year at Mansfield was hard. I had never been in a program with so much wasted talent. You might think that's a harsh statement but it's factual. I love those players to this day but I disliked the product that we produced and displayed. That year I had a group of six seniors. Three of those were some of the strongest leaders I've ever had the privilege to coach. For the others this was a way to finish out their high school careers and have some fun. That doesn't mean they were bad kids. They were academically sound and a pleasure to be around *off the field*. Unfortunately for those six young ladies I was their third high school coach in four years. There was nothing any of us could do to fix that but press on.

Kim Wallace was my assistant coach for the first two years at Mansfield. Kim and I spent countless hours in the coach's office beating our heads against the wall trying to figure out how to fix the program. We knew what the problem was but couldn't seem to chip away enough to make a difference. The problem was an individual mentality. We had quite a few *me over we* attitudes in the group. In a few cases it was *we over the team* attitudes. We had three main cliques on the varsity team alone. We were coaching a team with a social mentality and losing at every step.

That first year was the best worst year of my career up to that point. We ended the season 15-5-3 and made the 5A playoffs but I felt like a loser. It was a season that I could not be proud of. I will never be proud of winning on the scoreboard over winning the game of life. Coach Wallace and I made a decision that we were going to work hard every day to change the program for the better. Our focus was not on our play but our attitude. Our discipline. Our commitment. We were going to basic training during that offseason. A boot camp mentality is what we needed. We had clear expectations about everything we did. We scored and charted everything, and I mean everything.

The real mantra of performance follows attitude was about to arrive. Words we weren't just going to say but believe in and live up to. We used our previous season and real examples to show how our performance was only living up to our attitudes. That team wanted to be successful but they didn't want to do the things necessary to be successful. It's a hard truth to face but without honesty and true self, or team, assessment we were not going to change the face of our program.

When I graduated from the Air Force basic training at Lackland Air Force Base my graduating flight of Airmen was smaller than when we began the journey. You see not everyone was cut out for the life we were about to embark on. Some weren't strong enough. Some weren't disciplined enough. Some thought they wanted that life but found out quickly that it really wasn't for them. By the time my flight graduated we were smaller but stronger as a team than when we started.

Our boot camp at Mansfield High School wasn't meant to weed out players. Our intentions were to weed out the mentality that was holding us back. If we could do that and *graduate* our basic training with one hundred percent then we were fine with that. Unfortunately we lost a few during that spring offseason and a few more before the start of the next season. We left for summer break that year in a much better place as far as team attitude goes. For the most part we were nearing total buy in. There were still some with work to do but they were hanging on by a thread. When we came back from summer break we picked up right where we left off so nobody reverted back to the old ways. It wasn't long before Coach Wallace and I realized that we were going to be forced to make a few very tough decisions during tryouts. We were determined to begin the season with total buy in to the performance follows attitude mentality. We ended up cutting two returning varsity players and a third who was on track for varsity that year. Time after time we warned them and gave every opportunity to get on board. It was a tough decision but we stood by it.

During the course of that season those decisions were reinforced time and time again. I have never had so much fun coaching as I did that year and the next. The team was an actual team and everyone enjoyed each other. We didn't have issues. We simply played the game we all loved and we accomplished things that weren't even on the radar. We shocked a team who had dominated us the previous season. We beat them 3-1 in a tournament championship and the combined score the previous two years was 0-12. We had the same type of players, actually less talented in some areas because of what we lost from boot camp. The difference was the attitude of the players and the attitude of the team as a whole.

That team embraced the performance follows attitude mantra. They didn't just embrace it they lived it. It was so fun and rewarding to watch. They even dubbed it PFA, which has stuck ever since. They broke out of their team huddle by saying PFA. The girls would type #PFA in team group texts. Whenever they would pass me in the halls or field house they always said PFA Zell with a smile on their face. The same group for the most part but what a difference the attitude of a team makes.

After all of the successes of that second season, the best part of the year was in May. The season was over and I was working in my office one afternoon after school when I heard an unexpected knock on the door. I opened the door and there was one of the players who was cut back in December. She was a returning varsity starter and would have no doubt started that year as well if we were basing everything on talent alone. We sat down in the office that day and talked about her returning to the team. I was so happy! I explained how it was going to work and if she could handle it then the team would welcome her back with open arms. I stressed to her that if she came back not to put herself, the team, or me in the same position again because she knows now I mean what I say. She understood.

For her, it took losing something to realize how important soccer and the team was to her. Her opportunity meant returning to the team in August to go through the offseason leading up to our tryouts. I was clear that she would not make the team if she only showed up for tryouts. I wanted to see months of commitment instead of five days. Later that week I signed a schedule change for her and the rest is history.

I am so proud to say that she not only made our team, she earned her starting position back. She even went on to score the game winning goal in a playoff game versus that same team we had struggled with 0-12 for two years and then beat in a tournament final 3-1 the year before. We played them in the Area Championship game in 2013. We ended regulation and overtime in a 0-0 tie. It was a great game by both teams. It was a classic battle of girls on both sides leaving everything on the field. On to penalty kicks we went. Our captain took the first PK and missed the goal. That could have sent shock waves through our team but it didn't. We had been through too much together for that to impact the outcome. The girls had done too much to lose a mental battle. I had confidence in all of them. So we get to our fifth and final shooter only needing to score to win the game and move onto the Regional Quarterfinal. A goal meant the game would be over without the opponent getting their final shot. Our fifth shooter was none other than the girl who, against all odds, battled back from being cut the year before. I couldn't have scripted it any better. There's no doubt she was prepared. She had lost everything the year before and put in the difficult work to get it all back. She lost something she loved and found it again through sheer blood, sweat and tears. She was locked in. I'll never forget the ball entering the net and watching the entire team rushing out to her. The dog pile was on. The win was outstanding but even better was the victory that occurred with this team and in particular that young lady. She lost her junior year of soccer but with that gained a much more valuable life lesson. I bet she doesn't ever let something slip away from her grasp again.

That's PFA in a made for TV type of movie. Performance follows attitude is a mindset. It's a way of life. Living by the PFA mantra prepares you for anything life throws your way. If you can control your attitude you can achieve great things in life. If you aren't able to keep your attitude in check you will be allowing the most powerful enemy to emerge. That enemy is within us all. It's the part of humans that allows us to be weak minded. Controlling the enemy within means having a strong mind and a strong heart.

I believe it was motivational and inspirational speaker Les Brown who on once said, "we can only achieve what we can achieve." I believe in that statement wholeheartedly. We can only do so much. The problem with many of us is that we cap our own achievement. Our heart, our mind, our commitment, our attitude holds us back from being able to fully achieve to our own capabilities. For some, they don't even have a glass ceiling. It's fully walled off and they can't even see what's on the other side. Others have that glass ceiling and can see just outside of their limits but they are too comfortable where they are to break through. Those that break through go well beyond the ceiling because they are capable of so much more. They have a strong heart and mind. The combination of the two allows them to defeat their greatest enemy. That is the enemy within themselves. That enemy within is the builder of the ceiling. Defeat the enemy within and you will achieve what you once thought was impossible. Your attitude will lead you to achieve to your fullest potential.

The Mansfield team in my first year had a ceiling that was capping their ability to achieve. That team worked tirelessly between the first and second season to create an attitude of success and it paid off. The girl that was cut had a ceiling capping her ability to achieve. Over that next year she defeated the enemy within and you now know the result. The story was not about the wins on the field but the wins in the lives of young ladies who will go on to achieve at their full capacity in life, long after their careers on the field are over.

That is PFA at work and not just on a shirt!

6
THE PRESENT AND THE FUTURE

The life of a high school coach is much different than that of a club coach. Club coaches form their teams each year and have the opportunity to scout to bring talent to their team. A club team could change drastically each year or stay fairly intact. The benefit club coaches have is their ability to bring in athletes from anywhere as long as they are willing to make the drive or change teams.

High school coaches have a much more restricted method of building their team, or program. You get what you get in high school sports. There is no recruiting to fill holes in your program, or there shouldn't be anyway. As a high school coach you are going to have to coach what walks through your doors. I always loved the challenge and the thought that it takes to construct a team, and the program on a much larger scale.

What does it mean to lead today with the future in mind? That's very simple yet very complex. It requires a coach and his or her staff to honestly and continuously self assess the entire program. It requires an open-minded coaching staff. It requires time and energy.

The simple part is coaching, or leading, in the present. Having a plan for the day and doing everything in your power to coach as if it is your final day on the field or court. It sounds grim but imagine the job you would do if you knew it was the last time you would ever coach again. The last time you would ever be involved in the sport that you are so passionate about. The last time you would ever have a meaningful impact on the lives of young athletes. You would give it your all. Never sell your athletes short. Give them your all each and every day. You'll be amazed by the outcome of what such a simple change in you has on everyone that is part of the program. Whether it is a practice or a competition, coaching today means you have a plan of action. You have a desired outcome. You are well prepared mentally and physically. You have the PFA mentality.

I believe that many coaches lead with the present in mind. It is the easiest thing to do. Coaching in the present is normal. While many lead today, I do not believe that the percentage of coaches that lead as if it is their last day is very high. That is the first change everyone should make when taking an honest look at the way they approach their job. Remember that the job you have taken on is leading young people. What you bring to the table directly impacts the lives of many young athletes. As coaches, our most important responsibility is leading our athletes and teaching them how to win in life. Too often coaches believe their role is to *use* their athletes to win games. Don't confuse your responsibility with your desire. It's far too important a task.

My desire is for every coach to have the attitude of a champion builder. Play a major role in building future champions. Work alongside parents, teachers, and community members to develop young adults who are prepared to step into the next phase of their lives ready to conquer whatever life throws at them. Your job is to teach athletes that the process is more important than the result. For you to teach that you have to model that. If it's all about the W for you then you will be doing your athletes a disservice. As Brian Cain, a mentor of mine, would say, "Dominate the day!" Coach every chance you get with passion, commitment, and direction. It is a choice. It is a very simple choice. Dominate every opportunity to have a lasting impact on the lives of your athletes and others who look up to you.

Leading today with the future in mind is much more difficult. It takes more time on your part. Keeping the future in mind means more thought on your part. It requires you to honestly evaluate all areas of the program, including yourself and your schemes. The job requires someone with the ability to focus on the present while being able to plan for the future. High school coaches have to plan for the next year in advance so their offseason is meaningful. You have to think about potential changes that will happen in the future in order to find opportunities to provide quality time for those players in the present. You have to have the conversations with your staff about the needs for the future so you can communicate effectively with your athletes about their progress or changes that will be expected of them. If you don't plan ahead and have those conversations you are just spinning your wheels and coaching day to day with little to no future investment, much like living paycheck to paycheck.

So how do you coach today with the future in mind? As a head coach you must be intentional. You must have great vision. You have to think critically and be a problem solver. You must have a good open line of communication with your coaching staff. All staff members have to be fully engaged and committed to the progress and success of the entire program, not just the team in the program that they coach. It's coming in after practice or games and discussing players, systems, or what went right or wrong that day and knowing why. The coaching staff has to know the program inside and out. The staff has to be on the same page.

I was blessed with a coaching staff for most of my final years that was locked in and had a good understanding of what it meant to coach in the present while planning for the future. In the middle part of my career I was blessed with two young coaches who had a wealth of playing experience. It was great to bounce ideas off of each of them and help in their growth of seeing the big picture while building a program. It's funny how life works because these two coaches worked *with* me at different schools but in back-to-back years. Jena Lind was with me at Kennedale as a first year coach. You have already been introduced to Kim Wallace who was in her second and third year of coaching during our first two years at Mansfield. The funny thing is that these two young coaches played together in high school. They both went on the become head coaches. These were years that as a coaching team we were able to discuss strategy and the future but at the same time these young coaches were maturing in their own right. We were coaching in the present but with the future in mind.

My goal as a head coach was to never shy away from bringing in the very best coaching staff when given the opportunity. The opportunity is not always there as we discussed earlier. Sometimes your staff is pieced together because of the needs of other programs on your campus. When you have the opportunity to bring someone in specifically for your program you should not hold back. Seize the opportunity! Don't be afraid of the challenge of working with someone like-minded or even more experienced. A great coaching staff is a huge asset to a program and the lives of its players.

My final year of coaching was my very best from a staff standpoint. When coach Wallace left

Mansfield after accepting a head coaching position I knew exactly who I wanted but the timing just wasn't right. The opening happened in June and school was already out for the summer break. Jana Hammonds, a longtime opponent and friend, was a head coach at a nearby school and even though she very much wanted to come over and join the staff she just couldn't leave her kids. At that time, it was exactly the right decision for her and for her kids but I had to try. It was that decision that made her the right choice for the job.

She was coaching her kids with their future in mind. If she was coaching in the present coming to Mansfield was a no brainer. Not to be rude but her current position at the time was not producing winning seasons. She would have gone from one extreme to another if it were about winning. I knew that about her which is why she was so valuable to bring to my program. She would be a huge asset in our PFA mantra and with the changes occurring in our program, on top of bringing the experience of a state champion and coaching skill. She regretfully turned down the opportunity because she was winning in the lives of the young ladies in her program and on her campus. They didn't need the skills of an X's and O's coach so to speak. They didn't need the strategic thinker that brings technical and tactical vision to the program. It wasn't about that for them. Don't misunderstand, they wanted to win and they played very hard. Coach Hammonds brought those things for sure, but the other coaching she brought, life coaching, was much more valuable. They needed Coach Hammonds to be there for them. They needed a constant in their lives. Someone they knew loved them but still challenged them to be bigger than life. Coach today with the future in mind! Jana embodies that coaching style.

Coaching today with the future in mind is about preparing your athletes for life after athletics. Jana was a great example of that. Many coaches around the country are great examples of that steady figure in the tough lives of our young people. They work each day through sports to build a future for kids that may not otherwise have meaningful options for a successful future.

Coaching today with the future in mind is also about preparing your program for the future. It is meeting with the coaching staff. It is meeting with the players. It is constant evaluation of players and how their piece helps complete the puzzle. It is about a never-ending mental dialog about what worked and what didn't work. It's about the process of discovering why it worked or didn't work. It's not making excuses about what you don't have but creating the pieces out of what you do have so the puzzle can be completed. It's not getting in your vehicle and going home just because practice is over. The time spent off of the practice and game surface can be arguably the most important time spent working on your program. Obviously you can't spend a lot of time in the office thinking about success and hope it just happens. There is a process that takes place in every successful team. It's the show your work mentality. The stuff in the middle must be present as well.

It is hard work. I have seen many examples of programs reaping the rewards of a coaching staff with a present and future mentality. I have also seen just as many programs suffering because of their leadership, or lack of. Both are great examples of what it means to be a Program Coach instead of a Seasonal Coach. Seasonal coaches look forward to the end of the season because they get to go home right after school. They don't have anymore long nights of practices, scouting, or games. Coaches stuck in this seasonal mindset should be replaced because they don't have the future in mind for themselves much less their athletes.

You know a Program Coach when you see them because they are always working on their sport. There is no going home right after school when the season is over. They don't know how to turn the season off. It's not in their DNA. Program coaches can be found in their offices planning the off-season workouts. They are scripting the rosters for the next season, even though it's six or seven months away. Program coaches can be found in the locker rooms creating a culture for their athletes that encourages by in and a performance follows attitude way of life. There's no denying it when you see it. We can all label coaches that we know in our networks or in our area. It is a visible trait in our profession.

Make sure you are doing everything in your power to lead with the program mindset and with your athlete's future in mind. It's not about your future. Do things the right way and your future will take care of itself because of the body of work you are creating. I wasn't trying to bring in Coach Hammonds because she was a great coach in the moment. Her body of work made her so successful because she was a great coach and through her coaching mindset she led young ladies toward a future where success could be seen. Her athletes could envision a different life for themselves because she taught them the value of hard work, discipline, compassion for others, and the performance follows attitude mantra. In order for her to do all of those things she had to first prove to them that she cared about their future, not hers.

As Paul Harvey famously said during his broadcasts, "And now the rest of the story." I was never one to take no lightly. I am a competitor. When given the opportunity I am going to fight to make my staff better. Bringing Coach Hammonds in didn't happen on the first attempt because of timing. I left the door open and then began talking to her about the position again about six months later during a January game we played against each other. My assistant was not a soccer person and ended up going back to her previous position as a head volleyball coach. The opportunity was there earlier this time and I went to work. The timing was better this time around because now we were officially talking in April as opposed to June and, without going into detail, it just felt right for her to move on from the current coaching assignment at that time.

Jana and I coached together for one year before I hung up my whistle for administration. I would argue that we were the best two person coaching staff around. Not that either of us were the best coaches in our sports. I will say, and I know Jana would echo this, that we both had, and still have, plenty of room to grow. In order to be successful in growing a program and the lives of the young people in your program you have to realize your individual, as well as your staff, strengths and weaknesses. We were a great team because we each brought something very different to the program that worked to complete us as a coaching staff. We were both very competent coaches. More importantly, we shared a vision for our program. Our strengths complimented the others weaknesses. We each trusted that the other was always working on behalf of the program, not ourselves.

Those are important examples to include because coaching today with tomorrow in mind is not easy. Hiring young, up and coming assistant coaches can be challenging. Hiring competent veteran coaches can create a disturbance in the coaching office and ultimately in the program.

Make sound decisions for your program. Plan with the future in mind. Know what the programs needs are for today, next month, and the next year. Know who you are and who you are not! When you honestly evaluate the entire situation, then and only then will you be able to bring in the right staff to benefit the program.

7
OWN YOUR MISTAKES

One of the things people tend to forget about coaches is that we are humans. To be really honest, coaches themselves forget it, or choose to believe they are immune from making mistakes. Neither of those are a realistic way of thinking. People make mistakes. Coaches make mistakes. The key is not necessarily the mistake itself but what is done in the aftermath.

In my opinion, one of the greatest attributes a coach can possess is the ability to honestly self reflect and assess himself or herself. What a coach does next is very telling about the type of coach they are. I believe this falls right in line with the description of a Program Coach and a Seasonal Coach. Once a mistake is made you only have a couple of options.

The first option is to simply hide it or make some sort of excuse. This is the Seasonal Coach that is concerned about number one, himself or herself. Remember the Seasonal Coach is all about the W instead of developing the total student athlete. Seasonal coaches will find an excuse for every mistake. They will blame the system for their mistake. They will blame other coaches or parents. Even worse, they will blame players for a mistake because it is just not possible for them to own anything, except the W of course.

Imagine what kind of relationship this coach will have with his or her players. What will other staff members in the program, or on the campus, think about this coach? What are the athletes saying about this coach when they get home? Will the parents be supportive or will this mentality lead to further issues down the line because all they ever hear is negative?

The other option is to simply own the mistake and move on. There is no rule that says a coach can't make mistakes. It is going to happen. It could be about strategy or playing time or forgetting to send a message out to parents notifying everyone of team information. Things happen. The first step is to self assess and think about the entirety of the situation. This is where having a solid coaching staff can really help. Bounce ideas off of your colleagues and develop a plan to resolve it, if needed, and to move forward.

The Program Coach is going to be the type of coach that owns his or her mistakes. He or she is going to have discussions so everyone grows from the mistake. The Program Coach is going to take care of his or her players by owning a mistake to them. The parents will continue to be in this coach's corner because he or she takes responsibility for it. The coaching staff will know that it's ok to be wrong at times and that each member is valued because of the acknowledgement of a mistake.

In my experience as a coach I made numerous errors. In coaching you often learn about these after the games or practices are already over and they are too late to correct in the moment. You learn about these strategic mistakes through reflection after the game. If you are anything like me, a game or a particular event that has you troubled will weigh heavily on you and you just can't shake the mental process going on. My suggestion is to listen to the dialog going on in your head and have conversation with your staff about the problem. I believe most of what needs to be solved will come to you if you allow the mental dialog and reflection process to happen. Simply put, listen to your gut!

Once you have reached the point where you realize that you made an error of some sort then I strongly encourage you to own. Tell the party involved that the mistake is on you. Some mistakes will require more time than others. Weigh each situation carefully and take care of business. I promise you that the person, the team, or the group that is receiving the apology will respect the decision to own it and in the end the program will benefit. One of the rewards of taking responsibility is that all parties involved will recognize that it's not about you. You are not in it for the W. It is about life. It is about teaching our athletes how to be successful in life. It is about teaching our athletes how to fail and get back up rather than make excuses and stay down. Set the example for your program and watch what happens as a result.

Identify it. Own it. Move on.

I mentioned making numerous errors during the course of my career. I have several that stand out as key lessons for me as a coach that I think are worthy of sharing in hopes that others will think before they act.

This is one that sticks out and that I still think about to this day. I don't dwell on this because I learned from this set of mistakes and have moved forward. It was the spring of 2013 and my team had just knocked off what had become our mantra opponent. We used this opponent and our experience with them as the guiding force behind our transformation as a program. This was the team that had beaten us by a total of twelve goals in two consecutive years, the second being my first year at the school. That was the same team that we played in the spring of 2012 and beat to win a tournament championship. Now we beat them to win the Area championship.

Where is the mistake in that? It's simple. Everything we had done was to prepare us to compete with quality opponents but we used that one team as our driving force. We won the game and were moving on to the Regional Quarterfinal against an *unknown opponent*. Don't get confused, we knew them but we only knew them by name and reputation.

This particular mistake was more multi faceted on my part. Go big or go home I guess.

***

My first mistake was over preparing for the mantra opponent. I used the loss to that opponent in

2011 as our focus point. We were not going to be the team that got pushed around and dominated like we did that day. We were not going to be the team that was content with losing because someone was better than us like we were that day. We were going to be better. The issue was that team became our peak. We needed that push to be better but there needed to be a continuation to the top after getting through them. I didn't create that plan, in time anyway. I was too late for 2013. The players fought hard but in the end I had created a cloud that made it appear as if the mantra opponent was the peak when in fact there was more for us to do.

My next mistake became clear to me just before half time of that Regional Quarterfinal game. I had over thought the plan. I gave too much respect to our opponent and as a result not enough respect to my own players. In no way would I ever do that intentionally but I got caught up in scouting and out coached myself.

The leads right into the final mistake that evening and the days before. I should have trusted what got us to that game. I should have trusted my girls. I should have had the confidence in them that they so deserved. This was my greatest mistake of the evening.

So after that game it was my duty to tell them how much I appreciated their efforts and for what they had done for the program in such a short time. I also had to own my mistakes and fortunately I was able to do so that evening in the lock room. I was able to do so in the moment because I realized quickly the mistakes I mentioned. So I simply owned it to about twenty-five teary eyed young ladies who gave me everything I asked of them. I let them know that the result that evening was not a reflection of their efforts but my mistakes. I let them know that I loved their drive and commitment to excel. I believe being able to verbalize those mistakes are important in a program. Owning it gives you the ability to coach them hard the next time you are on the field or court. Owning it shows them you truly care about them and the program, not just the result. Finally, I vowed to never again lose sight of the quality of their work, their abilities, and the potential of the program.

***

Unfortunately I have made this next mistake several times. Do you ever get so immersed in a game that you overlook subs? I always had a basic plan for each game. Of course that depended on how the game was actually going that night. It's fair to say though that I typically knew which players would sub for starters.

We had the luxury at times to know in advance that we would likely be able to rest starters early in a few games. I used these opportunities to teach the team to get after it from the beginning and put teams away early. Once we accomplished that I used the opportunity to help us plan for the future. I would speak to my assistant coach and we would bring up a few junior varsity players in order to get them some varsity experience along with the remaining varsity bench.

This night I unintentionally substituted a junior varsity player before a varsity player. This varsity player was a great team player. She always worked hard. She always had a great attitude. She never once questioned her role on the team. She deserved the opportunity to be in the game and definitely should have been before the player brought up from the junior varsity. I just got caught up in the game and with the new additions to the team that night and simply missed her. I didn't realize what I had done until I was calculating the game stats and minutes played by each player. I couldn't believe it.

The next day I happened to see her in the school hallways before practice. She was with a few other players. I asked them if I could speak with her privately. I apologized not because she was guaranteed time but because she earned the time and I neglected to call her name when I should have. To me there is a huge difference.

I did not believe in having that conversation with everyone that wasn't playing in games. I had player conversations with everyone before each season and they knew their roles. This one however was my fault and I needed to own it so that I didn't lose her. I did not want her to question herself about why she didn't play or lose faith in her value to the team. If I had not taken the time to speak with her she would have continued to wonder why she wasn't playing. She would have wondered why I didn't value her more than the junior varsity player that played in front of her that night. That would have been a setback to her personally but also to the team.

My program knew from day one that playing time at the varsity level was never guaranteed. They were well aware that my decisions were based on the needs of the team, a players work ethic in practice and in games, a players overall attitude, and of course their ability. I was one to play work ethic and attitude over ability when the decision was close. Even with that disclaimer I still owed an explanation when an oversight was made. Owning it is so simple yet so powerful.

***

The one that haunts me the most to this day began as a way to spread more leadership opportunities and potentially grow players individually before leaving our program. Admittedly, one of these growth opportunities was a project.

I began the season discussing the leadership opportunities with Coach Hammonds. We had a wealth of options and tried to make a decision that benefitted the program as well as a few individuals. Before the season started we had settled in on two leaders for the team and agreed to consider a third option. I met with the third player with Coach Hammonds several times over the course of the first month of the season and put several requirements on her in order to fill the third leadership position.

My thoughts were that forcing this player to lead by example would give her the opportunity to see the big picture and allow her to grow before heading off to college. Honestly, I don't know if the choice was successful or not. I know that the desired result wasn't seen in the short time that she held a leadership role in my program. My sincere hope is that the conversations about what went right and went wrong during those few months will click at some point during her life and will open her eyes to the type of person she can be. Coach Hammonds and I were able to see through her tough shell and witnessed the type of person she could be when she wanted to. I personally witnessed her caring and compassionate side when she worked with special needs students in our school. That was a side she didn't allow many people to see. For her, that's exactly the person that she needs to allow others to see to be successful. It's the area of her life off the field that she does great, that she does the right way. When she approaches life in that way instead of small parts of her life she will do very well.

Even though there were struggles with my decision, I'm not ready to say it was a mistake. The process I went through during this selection was my greatest mistake. I had a returning captain but I chose to select another player instead to allow the opportunity for another player to lead. At no time was the decision based on one's ability to lead over another. It was simply to spread the growth opportunities in my mind. My mistake was not discussing my rationale with this player, especially after the decision was made to add the third captain a month into the season.

I was the typical male who never saw the problem. My first mistake was in making the decision without having a conversation with her so she understood. She was the type of person that no doubt would have understood the initial decision. The second mistake was not recognizing the impact it had on her after announcing the third captain. She was the type of player that would have never come to me about this. She just continued to plug away and get after it. Fortunately for me one of my players had the confidence to go to Coach Hammonds about the issue. This is where the balance of our roles benefitted the program so well. Coach Hammonds immediately earned the respect of all players in the program and they knew they could go to her for advice and direction. That's not something that most varsity players would do with assistant coaches.

Coach Hammonds immediately came to me to relay the problem that I had created. She informed me of an issue that I had not once thought about. She informed me that one of my players was hurting. This player had given the program more than I would have ever expected from a player. This player was everything I demanded and expected from them. She was one of those players that every coach would want to clone. I thought very highly of this player.

I hurt this player. The lack of foresight in this case created a sense of doubt in her. My mistake spoke volumes. My mistake relayed a message that she wasn't appreciated. My mistake told her that her efforts were not valued. Those feelings could not have been further from the truth but they were real feelings based on my actions, or lack of action in this case.

This information knocked me down. It hit me harder than anything I can remember in my coaching career. I coached my players hard. I always had high expectations of them. My players never really saw the soft compassionate side of me but I cared very much about each one of them. If we do it right, as coaches, I believe that we unofficially adopt an entire group of young boys or girls and they become like sons or daughters. I had hurt the feelings of one my own. That was tough on me, as it should have been.

The pain I caused her stuck with me all day until I had a chance to see her that afternoon. That day I delayed practice so I could work on fixing the problem that I created. I had to begin to mend the relationship that I damaged. At that time that was the only thing on my mind.

I called her and Coach Hammonds into the office and began to apologize to her. I saw her emotions for the first time and it made me feel just about the smallest I've ever felt. I listened to her. I felt her pain. The most important thing I could do in that moment was let her know how sorry I was for my lack of thought. I needed her to know that my foolishness was in no way a measure of her worth. I had to express to her that she was doing everything the right way and that I noticed. When I say she was doing it right I mean it. There is no better example of the perfect kid than her. She's the type of person, not just player that I would love my own daughters to model after. I was not going to let a stupid mistake on my part impact who she was.

We left that meeting on good terms and we continued on with the season. She was great as expected. She continued to do everything the right way and was a great leader for the program, and myself. I sincerely believe that we are on good terms to this day. I hope she knows just how much I appreciate everything she did for the program and how much I respect the person that she is.

***

It is impossible to go through life without making mistakes. The goal is to learn from each one so hopefully you make fewer and fewer mistakes. Keep in mind though; the most important thing is what comes next. Don't get stuck in the mud by pushing the blame off on someone else. You'll never get anywhere with that mentality. Successful coaches, or people in general, will identify the problem, own it, and move on.

8
THE COMPLETE PROGRAM

There are several ways to go about leading a program. A coach can choose to lead his or her players and that becomes the sole focus of what the program is. A coach can lead the players and the assistant coaches on the staff. Those two options are a good way to start for rookie coaches. As you gain more and more experience, or confidence leading a program you will need to incorporate parents and the community to build a complete program.

The players and coaching staff have been discussed previously but there has not been much mention of the other supporting groups that can make or break a program. Many coaches are afraid of involving the parents in the program because they feel like it is giving up too much control. On the flip side, many coaches don't even think about involving the community to help grow their program.

The Parents

This is one of the most misused groups in sports programs because many coaches tend to shy away from involving parents. Too often, the entire group of parents gets the reputation of the minority. We all know the vocal few that always speak the loudest. They are your harshest critics. Nothing you do can ever be good enough. I have been around quite a few teams of parents throughout my career and even now as an athletic administrator. Most of your parents understand the big picture and are great resources for you.

Don't shy away from getting parents involved. It's very similar to finding ways to delegate some of your responsibilities to your assistant coaches. The more little things you can release from your control the better off you are as a coach. If you aren't overwhelmed with minor tasks you will be able to focus on the major tasks. It took me quite a while to release control of things I should have never been doing on my own. Once I did I realized the importance of delegating. My mind was so much clearer. My time was better utilized. I ran with it.

How can parents help with tasks in your program? Every program is different and every sport brings its own types of opportunities. You will need to sit down with your assistant coaches and really think about what needs to be handled by the head coach, the assistant coaches, the student managers, and the parents.

What I'm seeing in programs today is an increased desire for a themed, or decorated locker room area. This is a great project for a group of parents that are eager to help. There is really no reason for a coach to be spending time decorating for the season, month, or week. Use your resources! I see a huge difference in decorating versus creating a culture in your locker room. I believe some of the culture building in a locker room is a job for coaches and athletes but game day decorating is much different.

Another area to utilize your parents is in different types of planning or scheduling of workers. Whether it's banquet design, concession stand volunteers, tournament workers, or even game day snack assignments, your parents can, and should, do this for you. Allow them to organize these functions and set up the sign up lists. They can be responsible for filling the gaps in assignments and sending communications out detailing the needs of the event. This will save you tons of time while creating a culture of inclusion in your program.

How do you get all of this established?

The first piece is to know your group and know them well. This is very difficult in your first year at a school. You don't know anyone and you really don't know his or her motives at this point. My suggestion is to observe everyone. Set up an early meeting in your first year with the program. This allows them to get to know you and, equally important, you get to know them. I held a meet and greet in the summer before my first year so I could meet everyone face to face before we got started. Take note of who takes the time to attend the meeting or who cares enough to send an email because they are unable to meet that particular day. Keep a running log of your thoughts as you meet everyone. Listen to what they have to say. Read their body language. Follow your gut!

Once you have an idea of who everyone is, start figuring out who would be great representatives of the model for the program. Depending on your circumstances, you will likely need a booster club president and other volunteers. If you do not have a booster club then you will want to find one person to lead your parent group. This is the person you will likely have the most contact with outside of your players and coaches. This person must share your vision or you could be headed toward a disaster. You need to trust that this person is communicating with the parents as if it is coming from you. Choose this person wisely! You'll be grateful later on that you did.

Once you've chosen the main leader of your parent group allow him or her to design the rest of the elements as he or she sees fit. If you have chosen the right person they will choose others that fit the model. Other examples of leaders could be locker room design, game day snacks, banquet coordinator, tournament and concession workers, and the list goes on and on depending on your program and the traditions in place or new traditions you are bringing in.

I have found that the more you include parents in your program the better off you are. Including parents doesn't give you a free pass by any means. Including them provides opportunities to build relationships outside of the normal times they would be around you like games, parent meetings, and banquets.

An established relationship with parents creates a group of allies that you might just need one day. That's not the reason for the relationship but it certainly is a benefit. Typically, when you have established the relationship with a parent a necessary meeting about an issue will go much smoother than a meeting where there is no relationship. It's just human nature. Meetings between people with a working relationship or common understanding tend to be much more professional and productive than meetings between two parties with no prior relationship.

As I sit here today I can tell you with certainty that you will not likely reach every person that comes through your program. Some people are willing to help and offer there time and others are not. Be open to understanding the difference between a parent that is unwilling to help and a parent that is unable to help. An unwilling parent just won't be available at all no matter what they are asked to do. A parent that is unable might have certain limitations. Figure out how to work around those limitations when needs come up that may allow them to be involved. Maybe for them it's just hanging banners at a game or transporting heaters or flags to games because they have a truck. There is a role for everyone if they want to be involved. Your job is to find it.

Your greatest issues will most likely come from a select few that don't believe in the program mindset. These are the one's that will complain about playing time or team placement because they are looking through the family lenses, a singular lens, instead of the program lens that shows the bigger picture. It's very similar to a team complaining about the officiating of a game. The officiating is probably not the problem. The problem is the coach, the players, or the parents of one particular team having tunnel vision. Everything is always against them when things are going bad. It couldn't be that there is cause for the calls to go against them. It couldn't be that they actually should not be on the best team or receiving the most playing time.

Your job is to handle these differences professionally and with understanding. Work hard to resolve the problems and verbalize your expectations so hopefully everyone understands what is needed to resolve the problem. Make sure the player understands what is needed from them in order to create an opportunity to play more. Remember that nothing is guaranteed. Your job is to guide them and help them understand what they need to do to lessen the gap between them and the players coming off of the bench first, or even the starters. If you can do that then you are doing your job. You won't win everyone but do your best to coach without animosity. You are there to create an environment for kids to grow. Keep that in mind as you work through difficult times and it will help keep you sane.

When situations get heated make sure you allow time for all parties to calm down before scheduling a meeting. Never meet during one of these situations without allowing some time to pass. Everyone is different but a general rule would be twenty-four to forty-eight hours after the issue arises. Always have an assistant coach present during the meeting. It's a good idea to have your assistant take notes for documentation purposes. You will be too busy with the meeting to take good notes. I like the model of the assistant taking notes so you give the parent your full attention. Hopefully your meeting is all that is needed to resolve the issue but sometimes the meeting will go above you to an athletic leader or principal. Having the assistant coach present and the documentation from the meeting will help when the stories of how the initial meeting went are very different.

Remember that the kids and the program are the most important aspect of your job. Do your very best to take care of them and the majority of people will see who you really are. Never judge the entire group of parents based on one negative experience. Piggybacking on that concept, never allow an incident with a particular parent to get in the way of the future relationship with that parent. More importantly, do not let an issue with a parent negatively impact a player. It's difficult but you have to be willing and able to put those times behind you or it will eat away at you and ultimately impact the players and program as a whole.

The Community

The community is the most forgotten resource in many programs. There are so many great ways to get the community excited about your program. The two main concepts are to bring the community to your program and to take your program out to the community. Both should be used at various stages of the season.

Bringing the community to you is fairly simple but will require you to check with your campus administration or district beforehand. The most common approach is to reach out to your junior high schools or the youth leagues in your area and invite them to the games. Be creative with the plan. Find a way to incorporate the younger kids into the game or just the pregame. The kids will love it and you have just created a vision in their mind of what they want to be like when they are old enough to wear those uniforms. This is also a great way to get your athletes thinking about and being role models.

These are really fun events. They can be slightly distracting to the routine of your game night but it is well worth it. Again, be creative in your planning to minimize the effects of the distraction. You probably won't want to impact the pregame routine of a game that will decide a district, or league championship. Those are times to host a youth night but keep them in the stands. Bring the kids down and have them be a part of the pregame when there is less pressure on a particular game night.

The reverse of the youth night is to have some of your players go to the games or practices of the youth leagues or middle schools. With the cooperation of the youth coach, have your athletes help run practices or jump in and work on drills with the younger kids. These are memories that the kids will cherish. The benefits are far reaching.

In order for the community to get involved in your program they need to know about your program. This is a job for the coaches but it can also be one of those areas where a parent is assigned to coordinate and distribute information. Create a poster with a team picture and schedule on it. This is also a great way to get sponsors. After checking with your district on sponsorship rules, just include their logo on the poster if you are able to. The next piece is to go around town and get business to hang the posters on the doors, windows, or a great advertising spot inside the store.

In addition to the posters, purchase extra program shirts and give to the businesses. Many of them will create a spirit wall for your school if they just have the resources to do it. Have your players sign a ball, helmet, old jersey, or anything else that ties into your program and give it to them. Businesses want to have the appearance of being supportive of the schools. It helps them gain customers and helps inform the community about your program.

Think outside the box when it comes to getting the community involved. Be creative and thoughtful and you will have success building the complete program!

A complete program has the undeniable leadership of the coaching staff, a visible passion from the players, and an exhilarating atmosphere of support from the parents and other community members. When you arrive to play an opponent with a complete program you know it. You want to model after it because even as an opponent you respect the excitement of everyone involved. A complete program is a championship program! Be a champion...

9
WHAT'S YOUR DRIVE?

It's who you are.

It's your purpose.

It's why you do what you do.

It's what keeps you going.

It's what gets you up when you get knocked down.

It's the guiding force behind a success... and failure.

***

What drives you? What is your personal and professional drive? Why do you coach? Who do you coach for? Identifying what drives you is crucial to success. If you never think about it you will go about your day just doing things without reason or passion. If that is how you approach your coaching, or life in general, you'll never reach the peak of your abilities. You'll be satisfied with mediocrity. As a coach and an educator you will be doing a great disservice to yourself and most of all, the student athletes that come through your program.

It's okay to not have all of the answers right this second. Be working toward finding what drives you. Think about where you want to be in your career. Think about why you want to be there and how you will get there. Think about the impact that your drive will have, not can have, on the people in your life. When you are processing all of that information the most important thing you can do for yourself is to be honest. Remember Honest Zell? I am my harshest critic. Embrace your honesty. Honesty is what will help you discover your drive and keep you motoring down the path of success.

The alternative is to be in neutral on the side of the road or worse yet, to be in reverse.

My greatest driving force is my family. They are behind everything I do. My wife is career oriented and managing two different paths that interest her. My drive can empower her to better and visa versa. Our focus as parents is ensuring that our drives don't collide with each other. We constantly have to keep our eye on the road and change lanes cautiously so we maneuver down the road safely for our kids. It's a joint effort. Our individual drive is also a parental drive. Understanding our drive has gotten us to this point in our journey.

Rachelle and I got married two weeks after I graduated and two months before I went off to basic training. We were kids with no real vision for where we wanted to go other than away from where we were. The one thing we knew was that we wanted to be on that trip together.

That was twenty-two years ago and here we are with our three kids. We have an eighteen-year-old son who is working on figuring out his path before graduation becomes real in a couple of months. Our daughters are fifteen and seventeen and full of energy.

It's funny how life works. It seems like it was just yesterday that I was getting on that flight to basic training. I remember that six weeks and then tech school vividly. Before long it was time for Rachelle and I to begin our life together. Our real journey began when we packed up and headed to our first duty station, Barksdale Air Force Base. We were two kids blindly traveling down the road. We had no clue how to maneuver down the path but we had each other. As time went on we began to see the path clearer and clearer. Different aspects of life helped show us the way. Life is a learning process. You just have to be willing to be taught.

I believe a turning point in our lives was the birth of kids. Prior to that we had each other but being a parent has a certain power that is just hard to explain. It brings a stronger sense of purpose. Life is no longer about you as an individual. It is no longer about you as a married couple. Life is about your children. Life is about the family you and your spouse create for you children. They are the greatest driving force for us.

I have my kids in mind at all times. Whether it's my family life, my work life, or the part of me that continues to challenge myself to grow. I do all of it for them. My struggles and growth opportunities make me stronger. More importantly, they set the example for my kids. With every life experience I continue to create a solid path for myself but I'm also laying a foundation for my kids to build their path. They have the advantage of being a part of, or witness to, my experiences. They see the drive and determination that it takes to be successful. They see the resolve and strength I have when I struggle with obstacles and tasks. My drive is to be great so their path is better prepared than mine was. My drive is to create an atmosphere and a home that is driven instead of one to drive away from. Family is what drives me.

As coaches we have our family and we have our coaching family. I would be misleading you if I said my only drive was my family. That was the purpose behind identifying my family as my greatest driving force. Coaches without drive will fall into the seasonal coaching spectrum. In order to do it right, in order to be a successful coach, you have to be driven. You have to know the who, the what, the why and the how. I intentionally left out the where. A coach with purpose and drive and that does all of the other things right doesn't care about the where. You've heard the phrase anytime anywhere. Coaches that do all of the little things are ready anytime to go to work anywhere. Your coaching drive accomplishes the process necessary to compete if you are doing it the right way.

Much like my family, I worked hard to set the example for the coaches and players in my program. You have to be there earlier than anyone else and you are always the last one to leave. You are prepared for everything from practices to games, meals to locker room organization, parent meetings to banquets, and teaching to scouting. Your program is witness to the hard work and dedication it takes to prepare everyone for the journey. There is no denying the work ethic. When we lead the right way our athletes will take notice and they will follow us. Our athletes and our families take notice when we aren't being the leader we should though too. Don't miss that because it is extremely important. You are setting an example one way or another by your actions, your drive, or your lack of action, or lack of drive. Don't lose the ones that look to you as a model. Do it right!

The drive we have in our coaching career should not be about winning games. Our drive should be to build strong young people with great character. Our drive should be to develop athletes with great work ethic and determination. Our drive should be to help them create a sense of purpose and drive of their own and for the program. Our drive should be help them pave their path so that when they leave our program they are well on their way to leading the next generation. Coaching is a very powerful career. Never lose sight of your ability to impact the lives of young people. When your drive is focused on building quality young people through athletics then the wins will take of themselves. The process and the outcome are far more important than the final score on the scoreboard.

Coaches love their athletes. They don't always think we do. Just like my own kids, I was tough on my athletes because I cared. Our kids, personal kids and our program kids, don't always see beyond the drive. They don't always understand why we are so tough. They often turn purpose or having the drive to be better into a negative mentality. They confuse our belief that they can do better with being negative. It is worth remembering though how they see your drive. I am as guilty as they come with setting high expectations and not allowing my kids or athletes to see how proud I am of their efforts. We need to find the balance between maintaining high expectations and taking the time to acknowledge the work they have done. What I learned late in my career was I could increase the demands when I was intentional about acknowledging them. I was able to push them harder than ever because they knew I cared. They knew I was observing their efforts and taking the time to let them know it.

Please don't confuse your desire to win with your responsibility to instill drive in yourself and the people that come through your program. Think about the most successful coach you know. Now ask yourself why he or she is so successful. Ask yourself what kind of character he or she possesses. Why has his or her program earned the respect of the sports community? In most cases, the answer to those questions is because the coach is driven. His or her drive has a greater purpose than the wins and the losses at the end of each season, or the end of their career.

The great aspect about drive is that you are never too young or too old to develop a worthy drive. It doesn't matter if you are a head coach or an assistant coach, you will have an impact on the athletes that you come in contact with. It is your responsibility to make sure your impact is meaningful.

If you didn't know the answers before, maybe you do now. Get to work identifying and evaluating your drive. Be honest with yourself during self-reflection times. Sometimes an accurate self-assessment will sting but you recover and build a stronger you in the long run.

As we conclude, I believe it is important for you to be able to answer these questions. They will help guide you in the process of completing your path and building a successful program.

What drives you?

What is the purpose behind your drive?

Evaluate your current position in your purpose. Are you moving forward? Are you stagnant, or as I like to say, comfortable? Or, are you moving backwards? Truly take an honest look at where you are in your purpose. Anything less is just you lying about what drives you or letting down the one's you say are your driving force.

How can you make improvements on your current path? If your path is bumpy you need to get to work to smooth it out. If it's smooth you need to get to work paving it. If it's paved you need to get to work striping it so your road is an even better guide for others who cross it. If your path is smooth, paved, and clearly marked then you need to work each day on securing it. A road unmonitored will fade. A road unmonitored will get potholes. A road unmonitored will cause havoc and ultimately deter people from using it.

Your drive will lead to a program worthy of modeling to others. You can create a program that does it the right way but you have to show up each day ready get busy protecting your program. Never lose sight of your calling. Never lose site of your drive and your purpose.

I look forward to seeing you on the fields or courts some day. Go ***Coach 'Em Up***!

ABOUT THE AUTHOR

Jay Zeller is a lifelong supporter of athletics. He grew up playing a variety sports but found his true calling in soccer. Jay enjoys to play, officiate and, most of all, coach the sport he loves.

His journey began in the United States Air Force and then took him back home to Texas where he became a High School Soccer Coach. Jay settled into the world of coaching and spent eleven years on the fields before moving into school administration. He now serves players and coaches alike in his role as Assistant Athletic Director.

Along the way, Jay coached Soccer, Volleyball, Football, and Cross Country. He also served as an Assistant Principal before moving into Athletic Administration.

Jay is a true believer in being growth minded. He continues to seek the support and knowledge of others that have paved the way.

Made in the USA
Coppell, TX
19 April 2020